DIARY

OF A
MINECRAFT
CREEPER

BOOKS KID

TABLE OF CONTENTS

Day 1

Dear Diary,

I suppose I ought to introduce myself. My name is Mervyn and I've decided to keep a diary to help me with my preparation for the Creeper Combustion Confusion Competition.

What's that? You didn't think that creepers kept diaries? Well, this one does. And yes, I can read and write thank you very much. I don't know why people think that creepers are dumb. If they listened to us, they would know that we were talking to them.

The problem is that we all have a bit of a lisp, so we sound as though we're hissing all the time, like thisssssssssssssssss and we talk really quickly. If you don't listen carefully, I suppose I can see how it just sounds like we're hissing, but we're not. We're saying "Come here! We want to be your friend!" and then we get so frustrated that people don't understand us that we blow up. It's very annoying.

Anyway. The Creeper Combustion Confusion Competition. You may be wondering what the competition is all about. Well, the clue is in the name. Every year, the creepers have a competition to see who can cause the most damage and chaos. My dad won three times in a row before he retired due to an unfortunate accident involving an ocelot, a carrot, and a large bucket of lava.

Don't ask.

As you can imagine, there has been a lot of pressure on me to live up to my dad's record breaking achievements. It's enough to make any creeper explode from nerves.

So I've decided to keep a diary so I can record my training progress. If I can come up with a brilliant new way of causing maximum damage, I'm bound to win the competition.

It's going to have to be super brilliant. Wesley has been boasting that he's got some ideas that are sure fire ways of winning.

Ha! Sure fire. See what I did there?

Day 2

Have I told you that I really hate Wesley? He's so full of himself and thinks he's going to win the competition so the rest of us might as well not bother showing up.

He says that he's going to cause so much damage that they will never hold the Creeper Combustion Confusion Competition again because nobody else will ever be able to do as well as he does. He says that he's going to make my dad's record look like a baby creeper trying to explode for the first time and my dad will run off into the forest crying.

That does it. Nobody makes my dad cry.

I've been thinking about what I could do that nobody has done before. I really need to surprise the judges. I need to do something that will go down in creeper history. There's a lot of pressure on me as the son of the Great Raymundo, but I know that I can do it.

If Wesley thinks that he's going to be the one to finish off the competition, he hasn't seen anything yet. I'm going to blow him out of the water.

Unless he's standing on land. Then I'll just blow him up.

Day 3

Dad came out to help me with training. I did my best to impress him. I've been working really hard and I wanted him to see that I was doing my best.

First I ran to a tree and blew up next to it. It fell over and took out the two trees next to it.

After I pulled myself together, I raced over to dad. "Dad! Dad! What do you think? Was that really cool?"

Dad frowned. "If you'd exploded over here, you'd have done twice the damage."

He moved over to where he'd pointed and exploded. He was right. He destroyed six trees with just one small explosion. Why didn't I do that?

Piecing himself together, he made his way over to me. "Remember that the judges are marking you on more than just how much damage you do. They're also looking for creativity and inventiveness, all within the strict time limit. Everyone knows the 'making trees fall over' trick.

We've all seen it a million times before. If you think you're going to win by racing around the forest, taking out all the trees, then you might as well not bother. That's a classic rookie error. Really, Mervyn. I thought you'd grown out of that kind of thinking."

I hated when dad gave me that look. You know the one. The look that says 'you're such a disappointment as a son. I wish Wesley was my boy.'

"Sorry, dad," I sighed. "I'll try harder."

I looked around the clearing. (Because it was a clearing now, since we'd knocked down so many trees.)

"Ooh! I've got an idea!" I went over to the stream. Looking at the water, I picked my devastation point carefully. "Watch this, dad!"

BOOM!

I tried to make my explosion as large as possible. When the dust had settled, I looked around, expecting to see a massive waterfall.

"Oh no. It didn't work," I pouted when I saw that all I'd done was make the river a little wider. "I thought the water would gush through the forest, taking out half the land and creating a pretty waterfall effect."

"Mervyn, Mervyn, Mervyn." Dad shook his head as he came over to me. "You should know better than that. What are they teaching you in creeper school these days?

You know that the rivers here are static. The water doesn't move. All you've done is made a hole in the ground. In fact, it's barely a dent. It hardly even qualifies as a hole. If I were one of the judges, you'd be lucky if I gave you a point. The competition isn't far away. I would have expected you to have figured all of this out by now."

"I'm trying, dad," I wailed. "Can't you give me some help? If you could just show me that move you did when you destroyed the main road…"

"I've told you before, Mervyn. If you just copy me, you'll get marked down and you'll make yourself look bad at the same time." He sighed. "Maybe it was a bad idea entering you in the competition. Some things can't be taught. Destruction is a basic instinct all creepers should have. It's that feeling you get in the pit of your stomach just before an explosion when you know that what you're doing is going to destroy the world around you. You don't even have to look at the damage you've done when you're back together because you know that your target is gone."

I nodded, trying to look as though I knew what he was talking about, but if I was honest, I didn't have a clue. I'd never had a feeling like that. The only time my stomach felt funny was when I had food poisoning after eating some rotten meat dropped by a zombie. I was ill for days.

"Let's face it, Mervyn. There's only one champion creeper in this family. Perhaps you should give the competition a miss this year. Train harder and go for it next year. You don't want to look stupid, do you?"

"I won't look stupid! I can do this, dad." I could feel myself trembling and I had to control myself or I'd blow up in my dad's face. He didn't like it when I did that. He said that his nose felt funny for days the last time I did it.

"Are you sure about that?"

Dad looked at me skeptically before turning and walking off into the forest.

I wish that when he came to help me with training he actually helped me with training.

Day 4

After dad coming to training yesterday, I was too depressed to do any explosion practice today. What's the point when your own father thinks you haven't got a chance of winning?

Maybe Wesley is right. We should just give him the crown and all go home.

I wandered through the forest, not paying any attention to where I was going. I was so lost in thought that I didn't even notice when I'd left the forest and was out in the plains. Up ahead I could see a village and I decided to go and blow up a shelter or two. Maybe that would cheer me up.

"Aargh! Aargh! A creeper! A creeper is coming!"

Usually the terrified screams of villagers would put a smile on my face, but I was too miserable to care.

I moped through the village, villagers running around me. Soon the iron golems would come and chase me away, so I didn't have much time if I wanted to destroy something.

A building caught my eye. Moving closer, I read the word over the door.

'Library.'

The library! I had an idea. Maybe I could find a book in there that would help me in the competition.

I went through the door. The librarian screamed and sped out the door as soon as he saw me. I ignored him. I was a creeper on a mission.

I moved up and down the aisles, looking for a book that might be useful. I found a section marked 'Creeperology' and I looked through all the books on the shelves.

How to disarm a creeper.

10 top tips to fight creepers.

Creepers I have known and destroyed.

The best creeper traps.

These were no use at all. This had been a stupid idea. Perhaps I should just blow up the library.

It was then I saw them. The books on building and resources. That was it! How could I cause the most destruction? By making things to destroy!

I quickly gathered as many books as I could carry, even putting one in my mouth, then I headed out of the library and back to the forest.

Tempting as it was to blow up the library before I left, just because I could, that could wait until another day. There was work to be done.

Day 5

If dad could see how hard I worked studying those books, he would have been proud. Well, either he would have been proud or he'd want to know why I didn't work as hard at Creeper College.

I had no idea you could make so much cool stuff! It's not just that you can build shelters. You can build entire cities!

As I read the books, my brain was buzzing with ideas. Maybe I'd forget about the competition and just go somewhere and build the first creeper city.

But then I thought about Wesley and how much he laughed at me all the time. I was going to wipe that smug look off his face once and for all.

After I'd read all the books, I turned back to the beginning and read them all over again. There was so much information in them that it was hard to take it all in. I'd need to take notes and start plotting.

For now, I hid the books by a tree, digging a little hole and then covering them up again so nobody else would find them. I didn't want Wesley to steal my ideas.

I was going to win this competition and then next year's and the year after that and the year after that. If anyone was going to break my dad's record, it's going to be me.

Day 6

"What are you doing, worm?"

I looked up to see Wesley standing over me with two of his cronies, sneering. Just my luck. I thought I'd found a quiet little corner of the schoolyard to sit and plot out my approach to the competition. I should have known that Wesley wouldn't leave me alone.

"Oh, just thinking."

"Nah, that's impossible. If you're going to think, you have to have a brain. No wonder you looked so vacant!"

His two friends burst into laughter with him. I started trembling and I had to calm myself down. We're not supposed to blow each other up in the schoolyard. It's not because they don't want any of the creepers to get hurt. It's just that it's a lot of work for the janitor to keep fixing the holes in the ground that it makes. Mr. Jungle is really grumpy anyway. He gets even worse when he's shoveling dirt.

I decided enough was enough. I was tired of Wesley teasing me. "You know, for someone who's so convinced that he's going to win the competition, you seem to spend a lot of time trying to put me off my game. Anyone would think that you were worried about losing. What's the matter, Wes? Scared?"

Wesley paled and I realized that I'd hit a nerve. "It's Wesley to you, worm. And I'm not scared of anything."

"Oh really?" I arched an eyebrow. "Well, it's Mervyn to you and if you're not scared, then you won't mind taking on a little bet."

"Name your price!"

"If you beat me in the competition, I'll do your homework for a month. But if I beat you, then you have to do mine."

Wesley laughed. "Is that all? Fine! I hate doing homework anyway."

"No, that's not all." Perhaps it was a dumb thing to do, but I was desperate to wipe the smug look off Wesley's face. "That bet is just for whoever does better in the contest. If one of us wins, then the other one has to wear a T-shirt that says 'I'm a big loser' and walk – don't run – around the forest shouting 'I'm a loser!' giving out rotten fruit for people to throw at you."

If Wesley's friends weren't standing right next to him, I don't think he would have agreed, but I knew that Wesley didn't want to look scared in front of them.

"I hope you've got plenty of fruit handy, worm. You're going to need it! Come on, boys. Let's go to the explosion yard and practice some more. We're going to show this loser how it's done."

Wesley and his friends went off in the direction of the explosion yard, leaving me shaking with nervous excitement.

What have I just done? Now I'm going to have to win. I need to see Wesley wearing that T-shirt!

Day 7

"Mervyn! Pay attention!"

Mr. Bing, our gym teacher, shouted at me, making me jump while all the other creepers giggled. "Right, Mervyn. You've just volunteered to go first. We're doing the obstacle course today."

I groaned as I dragged myself over to the start point.

"Remember. This is good practice for the competition. Now I want to see good, clean explosions and a quick recovery. You'll be timed, and the slowest creeper will have to do the course all over again. Are you ready? Go!"

He blew his whistle and I started racing towards the first obstacle. I was so desperate to do well that I tripped over a tree root and fell flat on my face.

Everyone laughed, Wesley laughing louder than anyone. "You don't stand a chance in the competition!"

I pulled myself to my feet, but I'd hurt my knee and couldn't run as fast as normal.

At last I finished the course, but it had taken me almost five minutes, and I knew that it would take a miracle for someone to be slower than me.

There was no miracle. All the other creepers sped round the course, Wesley even taking the time to stick his tongue out at me before blowing himself up at the end.

"Well done, Wesley," Mr. Bing congratulated. "That's your fastest time yet. I can't wait to watch you in the competition. You're going to do the school proud."

"Thanks, Mr. Bing," grinned Wesley. "I know that I can do the course even faster."

"I'm sure you can. However, it's Mr. Mervyn here who's going to have to do the course faster. Come on, Mervyn. You were the slowest and you know what that means. I want you to beat your first time or you'll be in detention."

I took a deep breath to calm myself as I lined up at the start of the course. I couldn't get a detention. I had too much work to do for the competition. The only good thing was that my time had been so bad the first time around that there was no way I could do any worse.

Yeah. It turns out that I could do worse. Just as I started running, Wesley called out to me "you're going to lose, worm!"

I got so distracted that I blew up, which meant that I had a time penalty. I was so fed up that I didn't put myself back together properly, so my foot went on backwards, making me even slower.

By the time I limped over the finish line, I didn't need to look at Mr. Bing's face to know that I was going to be in detention.

"Congratulations, Mervyn."

What? Had I beaten my time after all?"

"You've just done the course in the worst time I've seen all year. I'm disappointed and ashamed that any student of mine could do so badly. You'll be in detention for the rest of the week."

"The rest of the week?" I couldn't believe it. Dad was going to kill me! "But sir-"

"No buts. Report to me after class. No arguments."

"Told you that you were a loser." Wesley deliberately bumped into me as we headed back to the changing rooms, but I was too sad to care. How could I train for the competition if I had to spend every afternoon with Mr. Bing?

Day 8

"Right then, Mervyn. By the time I've finished with you, you'll never come last on the obstacle course again."

I groaned as Mr. Bing led me over to the start of the course. "You're going to run round and round and round until you don't know which way is up and which way is down. And then you're going to run round again. So get yourself ready and… go!"

I stood there, unsure whether I should run my fastest or pace myself. I couldn't believe that I was going to have to run round the obstacle course for hours. I was tired just thinking about it.

"What are you waiting for, Mervyn? Let's go. Step it up, step it up!"

Mr. Bing started running behind me, giving me no choice but to move as quickly as I can. "Time your explosions carefully and they'll help you move forward in the course," he advised. "And… now!"

I blew myself up on cue and when I was done, I realized that Mr. Bing was right. The force of the explosion had pushed me forward on the course and I was much closer to the next obstacle.

"Good job, Mervyn. And again. Explode… now!"

I did as I was told and by the time I reached the end of the course, I'd completed it in my fastest time ever. "Well done, Mervyn. It's good to see you make some effort in my class for a change. Shame it took a detention to get you to do it. Right. Let's go round again."

"Again?" I was exhausted, but Mr. Bing was a slave driver and, just as he said he would, he made me go round the course over and over and over until my feet ached and my head was sore from exploding so often.

"All right. That's enough for today," Mr. Bing finally said. "Same time, same place tomorrow."

"Yes, sir," I panted. Much as I wanted to be cross with Mr. Bing for working me so hard, I had to admit that he'd made a big difference in my exploding abilities, and that was just in one night.

Maybe getting a detention was a good thing.

Day 9

I never thought that I'd look forward to detention, but I couldn't wait for school to finish so I could go to the obstacle course with Mr. Bing.

When I got there, the course was completely different than the way that it was yesterday.

"Right, Mervyn. Since you did so well yesterday, I decided to switch things up a little. I've made the course more difficult, and you're going to run round it by yourself first so that I can assess your progress and we'll take it from there."

I lined up, ready to go. I was going to speed round this course and show Mr. Bing just how much I'd learned.

"On your marks… get set… go!"

I set off and for once, I didn't fall over. I was doing it! I was going to stomp all over this obstacle course!

I turned a corner and was faced with an enormous mound of iron. I was running too fast to go round or over it, so I had no choice. I blew up.

When I was myself again, I saw that the explosion had pushed me backwards. I had to run even further to get back onto the course and I'd lost a lot of time. I gritted my teeth and ran as fast as I could to catch up, but then I hit a slalom course. I had to zig-zag through tall posts and just as I got to the end, the final two were too close for me to be able to squeeze through.

BOOM!

Once more, I blew myself up and went backwards in the course. I was everywhere. One of my feet was right at the top of a pole and I had to climb up to get it back.

I could feel precious time slipping through my fingers. This wasn't good.

At last, I crawled over the finish line, exhausted.

Mr. Bing shook his head as he pressed the button to stop his stopwatch. "What happened, Mervyn? That was terrible!"

"It was the new obstacles," I protested. "I didn't have any choice! I had to blow them up, and that's what slowed me down."

"Yes, you had to blow them up, but you could have used that to your advantage. The course is designed to test you, but there's always a quick way through if you know what you're doing. Walk with me."

Mr. Bing led me to the start of the course and walked me round to the first obstacle, which he'd rebuilt. "When you came round the corner, you panicked as soon as you saw the mound. Don't panic! You've got time to breathe and figure out the best plan of attack. If you'd have come here, then you would have powered yourself straight through. Watch."

He blew up to show me what he meant and he was right. He went straight through the obstacle and halfway up the path.

"Now you try."

We put the pile of metal back together and I stood where Mr. Bing was pointing. "Face the mound," he instructed. "When you're ready, explode."

I did as I was told, closed my eyes and blew up. "It worked!" I laughed. "It really worked!"

"Exactly," nodded Mr. Bing. "Now let's move on to the next part of the course and let's see if you can find the best place to stand to give yourself an advantage."

Day 10

It was my last day of detention. I was actually quite sad about that. Over the past few days, Mr. Bing had helped me more than my dad ever had. I'd learned so much that was going to help me with the competition.

"Right, Mervyn. Tonight we're going to run you through a number of different courses, so each time you're going to have to think on your feet to make sure that you hit the mark on every single obstacle."

"Yes, sir."

I took my place at the starting line. I was determined not to let Mr. Bing down.

My first attempt didn't go well. "I'm sorry, sir," I panted as I reached the finish. "I did my best. I'm just not good enough, I guess."

"Don't say that, Mervyn. Don't ever say that. I never want to hear those words coming out of your mouth. You've got it in you. I've seen it. You just need to have faith in yourself. Now I'm going to set up a new course and I want you to run round it, thinking 'what would Mr. Bing do?' whenever you reach an obstacle. Remember, you have time to think about what you're going to do. You don't just have to explode the moment you reach an obstacle."

"Yes, sir."

"OK, now on your mark… get set… go!"

"What would Mr. Bing do? What would Mr. Bing do?" The words ran through my mind as I started off on the course.

The first obstacle was a jump. My first reaction was to want to blow up, but instead I paused and stepped back a little before throwing myself at it, leaping forward.

I made it! All the way over the jump and a few meters down the course. If I'd blown myself up, I'd still be piecing myself back together. Instead, I was racing off towards the next stage of the course.

The next obstacle was harder, a mishmash of planks, iron bars, and dirt blocks. "What would Mr. Bing do?" I whispered.

An idea hit me. I raced towards it, catapulting myself up and over the obstacle, detonating just as I reached the top.

The force of the explosion flung me over and down the course. Once again, I'd given myself a head start.

I couldn't believe it! I was going to get my best time ever on the hardest course I'd ever run.

"Well done, Mervyn," smiled Mr. Bing as I crossed the finish line. "That was an excellent time. You'll be on the school obstacle course team if you keep this up."

"Really, sir? You mean it?"

"Of course. I know talent when I see it. I've always known that you could do better than you have been in class. You just needed the right encouragement."

"Thank you, sir. I know detention isn't meant to be fun, but I've had a really good time this week with you."

"Yes, well, I know what it's like to have a famous father." He paused for a moment, wondering whether he should tell me. "My dad is Eric Bing."

"Eric Bing!" I gasped. "The obstacle course champion?"

"That's right," nodded Mr. Bing.

Everyone has heard of Eric Bing. He set the world record for the fastest obstacle course. He'd represented our forest in the international championships, and just when he was about to win his fourth title, a terrible accident involving a zombie pigman, a glistering melon, and some redstone put an end to his career.

Don't ask.

"I didn't have my dad's talent for obstacle courses, which is why I became a gym teacher, but you? I can see the same spark in you that your dad had. You could be a real champion. You just have to believe in yourself."

A little tear welled up in the corner of my eye. If only dad could hear Mr. Bing.

"Thanks, sir." I couldn't think of anything else to say.

Day 11

All that hard work with Mr. Bing over the week had made me determined to win the competition. He'd shown me that I had the ability to win. Now I just needed to put together a perfect strategy and the crown was mine.

I went to where I'd buried my books, but when I dug in the ground, they were nowhere to be seen.

Maybe I'd forgotten where I'd left them. I was sure they were under the tree to the left of the lake, but I could be wrong.

I started digging around all the trees, but there was still no sign of my books.

"Looking for these?"

I spun round to see Wesley holding up my books. "Did you think that you were going to win the competition by reading? You're even more stupid than you look."

"Give me back my books!"

I rushed at Wesley, but he held them up out of my reach.

"Don't be like that," he sneered. "I'll give you your books. You just have to go and get them."

He threw them into the water.

"My books!"

Wesley laughed and disappeared off into the forest while I waded out into the water to rescue the books. By the time I pulled them out, they were ruined.

I could have cried. Those books were going to help me win. How was I going to come up with an amazing plan now?

Day 12

Wesley had left me no choice. I had to go back to the village and get some more books.

I headed off. Now that I knew where the library was, it shouldn't take long for me to get together everything I needed.

However, as I drew near, I could see that the villagers had brought in more iron golems to defend the village. It wasn't fair. I hadn't blown anything up when I'd visited the library before. All I wanted was some books, but I knew that the iron golems weren't going to listen to me.

"Think, Mervyn, think! What would Mr. Bing do?"

And then I had it. This was just like an obstacle course!

I snuck around to the opposite side of the village. Picking just the right spot, I calculated the angles before blowing myself up.

BOOM!

31

Just as I'd hoped, the iron golems came running in the direction of the explosion. I'd picked the perfect spot to land right in front of the library. I knew I didn't have much time, so I quickly pieced myself together and zipped into the library.

"A creeper! Aargh!" I ignored the librarian as he ran away screaming, but I knew that I didn't have much time. He'd bring the iron golems back.

Luckily, I knew exactly what I was looking for and I headed to the building section. A lot of the books I'd taken last time had been replaced, so I grabbed my favorites as well as a couple of new ones.

A sudden impulse made me grab the book on creeper traps, just in case there was something in there I could use against Wesley, and then I was off back to the forest to hide my books somewhere really safe.

Day 13

I've been reading the creeper traps book. If I could just trap Wesley for the day, I could get some peace and quiet to focus on training for the contest.

The only problem is that most of the traps are designed to kill creepers. I don't want to kill Wesley. He might be really annoying, but that's a bit too far.

There was one trap that I liked the look of though. You set up a little room with doors on each side and lure the creeper in. You then lock the doors behind them and they're stuck!

It looked easy enough to make and once I'd had the idea, I couldn't think of anything else, so I started going round gathering the resources that I needed for the trap. It was a bit of a challenge without any arms, but I soon figured out ways of transporting the resources using my feet, and it's surprising how easy it is to move things along if you blow yourself up in just the right way.

It took a while, but eventually I had everything I needed and I started placing blocks and doors in the best location to trap Wesley. When I was done, I stepped back and admired my hard work.

"What are you doing, worm?"

Wesley! Just the person I needed. He'd saved me the trouble of trying to figure out a way of luring him here.

"Oh, just building a little something to help with my training for the competition." I tried to keep my tone light. I had to be careful with Wesley. He was suspicious and I needed to say exactly the right words to get him to step inside.

"Really? Looks more like some dumb doors that don't lead anywhere. How does it work?"

I couldn't believe it! Wesley was making it so easy for me trap him! If I led him in, then I could run round behind him and lock him in.

"Let me show you." I opened one door and stepped into the trap.

"Got you!"

I whirled round to see Wesley slam the door shut that I'd gone through, standing in front of it to hold it closed. I turned to one of the other doors, but his friends had snuck up while I was talking to Wesley and they were blocking all the doors.

Instead of trapping Wesley, he'd trapped me!

I could hear a rattling noise as Wesley moved from door to door, locking them all so I couldn't get out before throwing the key off into the bushes.

"So long, worm! Good luck finding your way out of that one!" Wesley and his cronies banged on the doors before running away, leaving me stuck in my own trap.

Day 14

It took me HOURS to get out of that creeper trap! The only good thing about it was the fact that the book was right – it really is a good way to contain a creeper.

In the end, dad heard me calling for help and came and rescued me. He wasn't very happy about it. He kept going on about how could I be so stupid and what was I thinking making a creeper trap?

I decided not to tell him that I'm planning on building other things. That trap was just the beginning.

Day 15

Sometimes I wish I had a best friend, someone I could tell all my secrets too. That's why I'm so glad that I started keeping this diary. It gives me somewhere that I can talk about my thoughts and feelings without someone laughing at me.

If I tried to talk about feelings with some of the kids at school, I'd never hear the end of it. It would be all "Mervyn's a baby! Mervyn's a sissy!"

You know, there are times when I wish I could be homeschooled, but then I'd have to spend all my time with dad, and that might be even worse. I tried to talk to him about my feelings once and he was all "Mervyn's a baby! Mervyn's a sissy!"

Sometimes you just can't win.

Still, ever since I had that detention with Mr. Bing, he's been really nice to me. It's funny because that was meant to be a punishment, but those detentions were some of the most fun I've ever had. It's almost enough to make me want to do something naughty and get more detentions.

Almost.

He's been giving me some more advice to help me prepare for the competition. He's told me that if I really want to wow the judges, I need to come up with something they've never seen before, something so amazing that everyone will be talking about it for years to come.

Talk about stating the obvious. Of course I need to do something amazing. Dad's been telling me that for years. I've lost count of the number of times he's told me about how he won the title three times.

One year, he lured a group of Minecraftians into the forest with a pile of gold and then exploded right next to them. That's probably why we never see any Minecraftians around here anymore. Nobody had ever used Minecraftians in the contest, so he got full marks for creativity. He scored 182, which was one of the highest scores ever.

Then there was another time when he set up a clever system that started a chain reaction when he exploded at the end of it. Trees, pigs, even hills all toppled over, one by one, just from that single detonation. He was lucky that his zone was set up in a way that let him do it, but, according to dad, luck had nothing to do with it.

"You make your own luck, son," he keeps saying, but I don't believe him. I'm one of the unluckiest creepers I know. Why would I want to make bad luck for myself?

Day 16

I hate Wesley. No, hate isn't strong enough. I loathe, detest, and despise him.

He stole my diary! Wesley the weasel stole my diary! As if that wasn't bad enough, he took it into school and read it out to everyone.

"Awww! Poor Mervyn! Does he have feelings?" he snickered as I tried to grab my diary from him.

"Give it back! That's private!"

I ran at Wesley, knocking him down, biting and kicking in my frustration. He rolled over with my diary underneath him so I couldn't get at it.

"Give. Me. My. Diary."

"Come on, worm. You're going to have to try harder than that." Wesley giggled as I did my best to get my diary out from under him.

"All right, you two. That's enough." Mr. Bing pulled the pair of us apart. "Now would you like to explain what's going on?"

Wesley looked at me. I looked at Wesley. Everyone knew that you didn't tell tales. But he had my diary!

"Sir, Wesley took my diary, sir."

"That's not true!" protested Wesley.

"Oh really?" Mr. Bing glared at him. "Hand it over, Wesley."

Huffing, Wesley passed him the book and Mr. Bing briefly looked inside. "This isn't your handwriting, Wesley. Don't worry, Mervyn. I didn't read anything you'd written. Although you might want to be a bit more careful about where you keep your diary in future. Wesley couldn't have taken your diary if you had looked after it better.

"As it stands, you both know the rules about fighting. You both have detention. Together. By the time I've finished with you, you'll learn how to work together and if you can't, then you'll keep having detentions until you figure it out."

He turned and walked off.

"You're going to regret telling on me, worm." Wesley stuck his tongue out at me. "Keep your stupid diary. It's not like you had anything interesting to write about anyway. Your life is as boring as you are. See you in detention, loser!"

Day 17

Having detention with Wesley is the worst. I'd rather be thrown into a pit of ocelots than spend another minute around him. He's so annoying.

"Right, you two. I need you to help me move the gym equipment around. First take that vault and shift it to the other side of the clearing."

Wesley and I looked at the vault and sighed. Those things weighed a ton and since creepers don't have arms, it's really hard to move things around.

"You go to the front, worm," Wesley ordered.

"No, you go to the front," I countered.

"I'm the strongest, so I should go to the back."

"I'm the tallest, so I should go to the back."

"Wesley! You go to the back! Mervyn! You go to the front! The pair of you need to stop arguing. There's a lot of work to be done and you're not going anywhere until it's done."

Wesley pulled a smug face at me as he headed to the back. It's not fair. Even Mr. Bing is taking his side now.

We went to our end of the vault and shuffled under it, standing up straight as we balanced the vaults on our heads. When you don't have any arms, you have to get creative in how you move things around.

"Move faster, worm!"

"I'm going as fast as I can! You slow down!"

"I can't slow down. I'll fall over!"

"Stop!"

"Keep going!"

"Aargh!"

Suddenly, Wesley dropped his end of the vault and it fell on me, bumping my head. "Ow! That really hurt!"

"If either of you damage any of my gym equipment, you're going to be in serious trouble," scolded Mr. Bing. "I suggest that you stop mucking around and just get on with it. When you've finished with the vault, I want you to move those mats."

Wesley laughed quietly when he thought that Mr. Bing couldn't hear.

"If you laugh at Mervyn one more time, Wesley, it will be detention every day for a month."

"But sir! The Creeper Combustion Confusion Competition is just over a week away. If I have detention I'll miss it and everyone says that I'm going to win!"

"Then you'd better behave yourself, hadn't you?"

It was my turn to laugh.

Day 18

I found a new place to hide my books. It's a little cave by the lake and I've put things around it to make it look like an ocelot den. No matter how much Wesley might brag about how he's not afraid of anything, I know that he's terrified of ocelots. All creepers are. Their teeth are so pointy and their claws are so sharp.

The more that I read the books, the more I think that creepers should build more things. There's so much interesting stuff that you can make. Why are we sleeping out in the forest when we could make comfortable beds?

I asked dad about this and he laughed at me. "Don't be stupid, Mervyn. Creepers don't need beds! We're fine sleeping under bushes."

"But dad," I protested. "Have you tried sleeping in a bed?"

"Of course not! I'm a creeper! I would never do such a thing! You need to forget about such nonsense and focus on your training. Creepers destroy things. We don't make them."

I didn't tell him that I'd made myself a bed in the forest out of wool and wood. It took me ages to get the wool. I had to time my explosions just right so that the sheep would drop the wool instead of blowing it up. It took a lot of practice, but I figured that it was a good way of getting ready for the contest. After all, Mr. Bing had shown me the difference a well-placed explosion could make.

I don't know why dad doesn't want to try a bed. It's so soft and warm, much nicer than sleeping on the ground. But I know that if I told him that I'd made a bed, he'd just get really angry with me, so I changed the subject and asked him to tell me more about his competitions.

Dad can talk for hours about his past victories.

Day 19

Ever since Wesley stole my diary, I haven't wanted to talk about my training here in case he did it again. However, there's nothing to stop me talking about his training!

I didn't mean to watch him practice. I was out in the middle of the forest looking for resources to build with. I'd seen a furnace in one of the books and I thought it would be a cool thing to build. If I set off an explosion in a furnace, it would send burning logs all over the place, starting a fire that would spread through my zone, destroying everything in moments.

After all, it is called the Creeper Combustion Confusion Competition and the rules just state that we need to destroy as much as possible – they don't say how.

I didn't find what I needed, but when I heard Wesley's voice, I ducked down behind some bushes to watch what he was doing.

"OK, guys. I want you to time me while I race around the clearing. I'm going to explode in each of the four corners, which should make this clearing twice the size."

I ducked down so he wouldn't see me as he raced past and I realized that if I stayed where I was, I'd get blown up too!

I crawled away, hoping that he wouldn't notice the movement.

"Ha, ha! Look at the worm! Crawling away on his belly, just like a worm should."

I froze.

"Trying to get some hints, worm?" Wesley came up behind me and kicked me. I rolled over and looked up at him. "I don't blame you. I am really good, after all."

He leaned forward and put his face next to mine. "But if you think that you're going to steal my ideas to win the competition, you've got another think coming. The judges don't like cheaters, and I'll make sure that everyone knows that you're cheating."

"I'm not cheating!" I protested. "I've got my own plan and it's better than yours."

"Really?" Wesley didn't even bother to argue with me. He turned and walked away, laughing so hard, he almost blew up.

Day 20

They've started putting together the zones for the competition, so half of the forest is closed off. I wish I could go and have a look at what they're doing, but I'm not allowed. It's strictly forbidden for competitors to visit their zones until the competition starts and anyone who tries to get a sneak peak at their zone will be immediately disqualified.

I wonder what mine's going to be like. I hope it has lots of trees in it. You can make a lot of things out of wood, and I have an idea that's going to blow everyone away!

Sometimes I'm so funny, I can't stop laughing at myself.

Day 21

It's really hard to concentrate at school with all the noise from the zone building, so Mr. Bluebottle said that we could have a break from work and play games in the schoolyard instead.

"Wesley! Clyde! You're team captains," Mr. Bing barked. "Take turns and pick out your team."

I hated when they picked teams like this. I was always picked last and sure enough, when it was down to me and Glen, Wesley picked Glen over me, even though everyone knows that Glen can't run and he can't blow himself up properly. Whenever he tries, he just sneezes and then a leg falls off.

"Right, Melvyn. You're on Clyde's team. We're playing dodgeball. Now remember, this game is designed to help you develop control over your detonations. Any creeper who blows up will lose a point for their team. Blow up three times and you're on the bench for good. Wesley's team is first. Get in position and go!"

I hate dodgeball. Wesley always aims straight for me, and he's really good with the ball. I was almost tempted to blow myself up just to get out of playing, but I knew that the rest of my team would be really annoyed with me for losing them three points.

Wesley aimed the ball straight at my head. I did my best to duck out of the way, but he got me.

BOOM! I couldn't help myself. I blew up.

"Melvyn! You've lost your team a point! You're out."

I slunk over to the bench, ignoring the dark looks from the rest of my team.

I wish Mr. Bluebottle hadn't canceled our lessons. I'd rather be in math doing calculus than out here with Wesley hurling balls at me.

Day 22

"Look behind you, Mervyn! An ocelot!"

"Aargh!" I didn't wait to turn around and look, and there was no time to find somewhere to hide. I blew up, hoping that I'd take the ocelot with me.

I felt like an idiot when I was back together again. Of course there wasn't an ocelot. If one had come into the forest, the creeper alarm would have gone off, warning us all to take shelter.

"You're so dumb, worm!" Of course it was Wesley and his friends. "I almost wish that I'd waited until the competition to try that trick on you. It would have been hilarious seeing you blow up the judges. But did you see the look on his face? Funniest thing I've seen all day!"

I flushed bright green as Wesley and his friends surrounded me, chanting "Ocelots! Ocelots! Ocelots! Ocelots!"

"That's enough! Break it up!" Mr. Bing came into the middle of the group. Instantly, they shut up, as he looked around at them all sternly. "Would somebody care to tell me what that was all about?"

"Oh, we were just trying to help Mervyn with his training, sir," said Wesley innocently. "He said that he needed help dealing with the unexpected, so we were pretending that an ocelot had wandered into the forest."

"Is this true, Mervyn?"

I glanced over at Wesley, who shook his head in warning at me. "Yes, sir," I sighed. "I'm getting nervous about the contest, so I wanted to make sure that I could stay calm, no matter what happens."

Mr. Bing looked suspiciously from me to Wesley and I knew that he didn't really believe me, but there wasn't anything he could do if I wasn't going to tell him the truth.

"All right. If that's what you've been doing, then keep up the training. Just make it a little quieter in future, all right?"

"Yes, sir," we all chorused, as Mr. Bing walked off.

"Good job keeping your mouth shut, worm," sneered Wesley. "We all know what happens to tattle tales round here."

I rolled my eyes and shook my head. "You know, Wesley. If I were you, I'd focus more on getting ready for the competition than worrying about what I'm doing."

Wesley laughed. "Stupid worm! I'm more ready for this competition than you could ever imagine. You're the one who should be worried about what you're doing."

I had a horrible feeling that he was right.

Day 23

"Come on, Mervyn. I want you to show me how you're going to win the competition." Dad led the way to a part of the forest that I didn't go to very often.

I couldn't believe my eyes when I saw that he'd set up my very own zone to practice in. "This is a re-creation of my zone when I won the third time. You remember what I did, don't you?"

Remember? I couldn't exactly forget when dad was constantly telling me the story about how he'd jumped from hilltop to hilltop, setting off explosions in quick succession to flatten the ground before running into the center and burrowing deep into the ground so that by the time he'd finished, the zone was the exact opposite of when he'd started, hills transformed into valleys and valleys into hills.

"I don't want you to do that. I want you to come up with your own way of using the zone. After all, it's possible that you may get the same layout, and you'll lose points if you just copy me."

"Yes, dad."

"Are you ready? On your mark… get set… go!"

I paused, doing what Mr. Bing had taught me, taking a moment to breathe and get a feel for the land.

"What are you waiting for, boy? Get a move on!"

I rushed forward into the middle of the zone and detonated. I barely made a dent in the ground.

Kicking myself for wasting time, I moved over to one of the hills and lay down at the base, thinking that if I could detonate there, I'd cause a landslide.

All I did was make a couple of pebbles jump.

Dad came rushing over to me. "Stop, stop, stop! I can't watch anymore. I can't believe that I let you enter a competition that you're clearly not ready for."

"But dad, I've got a plan!" I protested. "I just don't want to show it to anyone in case someone steals my idea."

"Don't be silly, Mervyn. There's no way you have an idea that's so amazing anyone would want to take it. You're just making excuses for the fact that you missed the obvious detonation points here and here." He moved over to where he was indicating and blew up, causing ten times the destruction my little explosions had made.

"Sorry, dad." I hung my head, pouting.

"Don't apologize to me. Apologize to all my fans who are waiting for my son to show them how great he can be. You're going to disappoint a lot of people if you think that this is good enough for the competition. Gah!"

He stormed off, leaving me behind.

Am I doing the right thing, waiting until the contest to test my plan? Maybe I should have practiced more and not worried about Wesley spying on me.

Oh well. It's too late to do anything about it now.

Day 24

The competition starts tomorrow and I'm so nervous, I've exploded four times already. The first time was at the breakfast table while we were eating. Dad was so cross with me that he sent me outside, telling me not to come back until I'd got my detonations under control.

"How do you think you're going to win tomorrow if you can't even eat breakfast without exploding?" he raged. "Keep this up and you won't even place. I warn you now – if you disgrace me, I will not be happy. You've got my legacy to maintain and I won't be embarrassed by my son."

Gee, thanks dad. Talk about adding extra pressure I don't need.

I went for a walk in the forest to try and calm down. Usually going down to the lake relaxes me, but as I drew near, I could hear the sound of Wesley and his friends laughing, so I turned around and walked the other way. The last thing I needed was to see him today.

How can he be so relaxed when the contest is in the morning? It's his first time entering too. I would have thought he'd be at least a little bit nervous.

Still, I guess he's got his friends with him telling him how great he's going to be. Nobody seems to think that I'm going to do well. If my plan doesn't work, then they'll be right, but I know that it's a good idea, even if no creeper has ever tried to do what I'm going to do tomorrow.

It's difficult to practice. Without knowing what's in my zone, I can't figure out the best use of resources, but I've been reading my library books over and over until I can recite them off by heart and I know that if I keep cool and take my time to get a feel for my zone, I'll make competition history.

Day 25

"Ladies and gentlemen, boys and girls, welcome to the 102nd Annual Creeper Combustion Confusion Competition!"

A cheer rose up from the crowd as Edward Higgins announced the start of the contest. Lined up with the other contestants, I jogged from foot to foot nervously as I waited for the start of the contestant parade. We would make our way all around the forest, past all the competition zones so we could see them for the first time.

"It's not too late to back out, worm," jeered Wesley. "You look like you need your mommy. Maybe you should just leave now before you make yourself look stupid. Since I'm feeling generous, I'll even forget about our bet if you go. You're not going to get a better deal than that, so I suggest you take it."

"Why? Worried that you're going to lose?" I shot back.

Wesley opened his mouth to say something, but he was interrupted by the sound of creepers exploding, sending bursts of fireworks into the air. The parade had started!

I couldn't believe that I was finally part of the competition. I'd dreamed of this moment all my life. I smiled and waved at the watching crowds as we made our way round the forest and all the different zones of the competition, each one assigned to a different competitor.

When we reached my zone, Wesley laughed. "There's nothing there for you to destroy! You should have backed out when you had the chance."

Looking around, I could see what he was talking about. My zone wasn't exactly what I would have liked. There was a lot of rubble in it and the entrance to an abandoned mine would be a problem for most creepers. Still, with my plan I knew I could make it work, so I put on a brave face. "Speak for yourself, Wesley. Just because you haven't got the talent to win doesn't mean that I don't."

The parade ended with a large feast for all the competitors, but despite the delicious food on display, I was far too nervous to eat anything.

"What's wrong, worm? Having second thoughts?"

I glanced over at Wesley, who was stuffing his face with pumpkin pie. "Just enjoy your dinner," I advised. "Because in a few days, you're going to be eating humble pie."

"You wish!" Wesley tossed a piece of pie at me and it landed right in my face. I narrowed my eyes, hissing at him, but I restrained myself from throwing something back. Knowing my luck, I'd get blamed for starting a fight, even though it was Wesley who'd started it. Then I'd be disqualified from the contest before I'd had a chance to show everyone what I could do.

Day 26

There were so many competitors, the contest lasted for three days. Our running order was chosen at random and I pulled the very last slot.

"That's good," Dad told me. "It means you get to see what everyone else has done and how much you need to score to take the title. The creeper who goes first never wins. I pity the poor creeper who gets that slot."

Dad and I watched from the sidelines as one creeper after another went out of their way to impress the judges.

"There are a lot of talented creepers here," I gulped as I watched one create an enormous crater where a hill used to be with just one explosion. "I didn't realize that everyone would be so good."

"What did you expect, Mervyn?" dad replied. "This is the Creeper Combustion Confusion Competition. Only the best of the best compete." He turned to look at me. "Are you sure that you want to do this? It's not too late to withdraw. There's always next year, you know."

First Wesley and now dad. Didn't anyone want to see me take part in the contest?

At the end of the first day, the competition was tight, with only five marks separating the highest scoring three creepers. "Our early leader is Marcus Twinkle," Edward Higgins told the excited crowd. "Will anyone be able to beat his score of 168? We'll find out tomorrow."

Day 27

Today was Wesley's turn and I watched him take his place at the edge of his zone. Was it my imagination or did he look a little more green than usual?

"On your mark… get set… go!"

At the sound of the starting gun, Wesley exploded! The crowd laughed and I felt a lot more relaxed. If he was so nervous that he blew up at the slightest sound, then he wasn't going to do very well.

I was going to win our bet after all.

Wesley pulled himself together and started to race round his zone. My heart sank as I watched him go. He might have started badly, but he was making up for lost time and by the time he'd finished, his zone was completely flattened and there was nothing left for him to destroy – with ten minutes still left on the clock.

"He'll get bonus points for that," dad told me. "That was very impressive – almost as fast as I used to be."

Of course, nobody would ever be quite as good as dad used to be, but it was very worrying hearing him praise Wesley like that.

"And at the end of Day Two of the Creeper Combustion Confusion Competition, Wesley Kerfuffle is the clear leader with a total score of 198 out of a possible 200," announced Edward Higgins. "Tomorrow's contestants are going to have a real battle to beat that score."

"Told you that you should have left the competition while you had the chance," jeered Wesley as he pushed past me. "But don't worry. I've got your T-shirt ready and waiting for you, and I've been saving fruit for weeks. By the time I'm done, you'll be dripping in rotten fruit juice."

He disappeared off into the crowd, surrounded by admiring fans. The way they were all behaving, you'd think that Wesley had won the contest already and with a score like that, he probably has.

Day 28

I didn't get any sleep last night. I was tossing and turning, thinking about what I was going to do in the contest. I'd been planning this for ages and now that the day had finally arrived, I couldn't help but think that my plans were stupid. There was no way I was going to win.

What was worse was that I was the last contestant of the day, so I had to watch all the other contestants try and fail to beat Wesley's score. Some of them had been competing for years and they really knew their stuff. If those talented creepers couldn't beat Wesley, what chance did I have?

"And now for our final contestant," called Edward Higgins. "Please welcome to the arena the son of the Great Raymundo – Mervyn Miles!"

Everyone cheered and I froze in fear. Why did he have to remind everyone who my dad is? Now I'm going to look even more stupid when I mess up.

"Go on, Mervyn. Get into position." Dad pushed me forward and at last, I found my feet and went up to the entrance to the mine.

"On your mark... get set... go!"

As the starting gun went off, I darted down into the mine, causing a concerned mutter to come up from the crowd. Usually, when a creeper has a mine in his zone, he blows up the entrance to block it up. You can get a lot of points that way.

I had bigger plans though.

I knew exactly what I was looking for, but I didn't know if I could find it in time. We weren't allowed to explore our zones before the contest started, so I was just going to have to hope that I could find what I needed before my time ran out.

I raced through the mine, deeper and deeper. "Come on, come on, where are you?"

It was no good. The resources I needed weren't here. I knew it was unlikely that I'd find some leftover TNT. Imagine how big the blast would be if I blew up on top of a pile of TNT! However, I had hoped to find some redstone or diamonds.

As it was, this mine had been abandoned for a reason. Everything useful had already been taken. There was no way that I could win, but at least I could get a few points if I destroyed some trees.

I was just about to give up and go back out again when I realized that the answer I needed was staring me right in the face. All the books I'd read had talked about what you could make with the most basic of resources, but I'd been so hung up on trying to create something unusual that I'd missed the most obvious.

Cobblestone!

I calculated the best place to detonate and took up my position.

BOOM!

I shot out of the mineshaft, soaring high in the sky, like a firework. I could see the other creepers staring up at me, their mouths wide open in awe.

When I hit the ground, I started racing around, putting together the cobblestones. No creeper in the history of the Creeper Combustion Confusion Competition had ever built anything, and the usually noisy crowd was completely silent as they watched me build a cobblestone castle.

When I completed my castle, I glanced over at the clock. There wasn't much time to put the rest of my plan in action, so I didn't waste a second admiring my work. I ran inside and stood in the middle of the courtyard ready to detonate.

This was not going to be any ordinary explosion. I had big plans for my castle.

I started spinning around letting the energy build and build and build before I finally let it erupt in the biggest explosion I'd ever created.

BOOM! BANG! BOOM!

My castle fell to pieces, the stones flying high in the sky before landing to create a beautiful stone garden.

I picked a flower from nearby and placed it on top of the stones just before the buzzer sounded to mark the end of my turn.

I turned to bow to the audience.

Silence.

This was not the reaction I was expecting.

Then suddenly everyone started cheering and hollering.

"Well done, Mervyn!"

"Good job, Mervyn!"

"You're the winner, Mervyn!"

I blushed and turned to look over at the judges, who were ready to announce my score.

"And Mervyn Miles' score is… 197 out of a possible 200. The winner of this year's Creeper Combustion Confusion Competition is Wesley Kerfuffle!"

My heart sank. Wesley won? After all that effort, Wesley had still beaten me?

"Bad luck, worm," sneered Wesley as he shoved past me to accept his crown.

Mr. Bing had been one of the judges and he came over to find me. "I'm so sorry, Mervyn," he said. "I tried to convince the others that you should win, but one of the judges marked you down because you made things. It didn't matter to him that you'd destroyed an entire castle, something no creeper has ever done in the contest. You built the castle and then left a garden behind, and he took marks off your score for that. You should be proud of yourself though. You've done really well."

"Not well enough though," muttered dad, standing behind me.

I couldn't help but agree with him.

Day 29

'I'm a big loser.' I looked miserably at the words written across the front of the T-shirt. Why did I ever make that stupid bet? It was bad enough that I was going to have to put up with Wesley going on about how he'd won the competition for the rest of the year. Now I was going to have to go all the way through the forest while everyone laughed at me.

Pulling it over my head, I sighed and headed out to find Wesley.

Dad came rushing up. "What are you doing wearing that ridiculous shirt? Take it off at once!"

"I can't," I replied. "I made a bet with Wesley. He won the competition so I have to wear this."

"What are you talking about? Haven't you heard?"

"Heard what?"

"Wesley cheated! He went round his zone before the competition and he figured out the best way to use his resources for the biggest explosions. He's been disqualified. You're the winner, Mervyn! You won!"

I could hardly dare to believe it. I ripped the T-shirt off and followed dad out to where the judges were waiting. "Mervyn!" smiled Mr. Bing. "It is my pleasure to declare you the true winner of this year's Creeper Combustion Confusion Competition."

"How? I mean, I don't understand. How did Wesley cheat?"

"He disguised himself as one of the workers and went to his area so that he could plan out the most efficient way of destroying it. I must admit, that I had my suspicions when he did so well. Wesley has always been good in training, but he was never that good – it was you who always had that inventive flair, a way of looking at things that nobody else would even consider."

"But how did he get found out? He must have been to his zone ages ago. Why did it take so long for him to get discovered?"

"Wesley is his own worst enemy," Mr. Bing explained. "You're right – he should have got away with it. If he could only keep his mouth shut, he'd still be the champion, but he just couldn't keep quiet. One of the judges heard him boasting to his friends about how he'd figured out that if he detonated at the perfect place, it would take out half of his zone, but he'd almost ruined everything when he blew up by accident. He said that if he hadn't been able to walk through the zone before the competition, he would have never noticed that particular point, and all the other creepers were really stupid for not doing the same."

"Wow. I never thought that Wesley would do that."

"What – cheat or tell everyone he cheated?"

I grinned with Mr. Bing. "Both."

"Well, he did and now the best creeper has won. Come on. Everyone is waiting for you over at the award platform. It's time you got the prize you deserve. That castle was amazing, you know. It almost seems a shame that you had to destroy it. Maybe you could show me how you did it one day."

"I'd love to."

Mr. Bing led me to the award platform where Edward Higgins and the other judges were waiting for me. As Edward placed the winner's crown on my head, I thought I would burst with happiness, but that wasn't the end of it.

"Now that we've had a chance to look at the scores in detail, you should also know that you join your dad as a record breaker," he told me. "You scored more 10 out of 10s than any other contestant in the history of the competition."

Dad came over and clapped me on the back. "Well done, son. I'm proud of you."

I never thought I'd hear him say that. I was the happiest creeper alive.

Day 30

Winning the Creeper Combustion Confusion Competition is the best feeling in the world. As I moved through the forest, I felt as though I was walking on air! Everyone I saw wanted to stop me and say hello and get my autograph, so it took a whole hour to get to school instead of five minutes.

As I walked into the school gates, the school principal, Mr. Bluebottle was there to greet me.

"Melvyn," he smiled. "Our prize pupil. I have declared today a holiday in celebration of your victory."

When the other students heard this, they all cheered. "Hooray for Melvyn!"

I looked around at the happy, smiling faces, but someone was missing.

"Where is Wesley?" I asked.

Mr. Bluebottle scanned the crowds, a puzzled smile on his face. "He's not here. I wouldn't be surprised if he'd left the forest out of shame for having been caught cheating."

I was a little disappointed that Wesley hadn't stuck around to keep up his side of our bet, but I couldn't blame him. I would want to leave town if I'd been caught cheating and if he really had gone forever, then that was even better. I'd never have to put up with him calling me 'worm' ever again.

I didn't have time to worry about Wesley though, as the other creepers lifted me up on their shoulders and carried me around the schoolyard, chanting my name. "Melvyn! Melvyn! Melvyn!" There was even talk of making a statue of me and putting it up in the middle of the schoolyard so everyone could remember my amazing castle.

I was the most popular creeper in school. I couldn't stop grinning. If they thought that what I'd done was amazing, just wait until they saw what I've got planned for next year's competition!

54249183R00047

Made in the USA
San Bernardino, CA
11 October 2017